Boeing 747-100/200
InCamera Vol 2

Scott Henderson

Airways
A GLOBAL REVIEW OF COMMERCIAL FLIGHT

© 1998 Scott Henderson

Previously published by Scoval Publishing Limited, PO Box 36, Ponteland, Newcastle upon Tyne, NE20 9WE, England

Library of Congress Cataloging in Publication Data available

ISBN: 0-9653993-3-8

All rights reserved. No part of this publication may be reproduced, stored in a retrieval system or transmitted, in any form or by any means, electronic, mechanical, photocopying, recording or otherwise, without the prior permission of the copyright holder.

Published by:
Airways International Inc.
PO Box 1109
120 McGhee Road
Sandpoint
ID 83864
USA
Tel: 1 208 263 2098
Fax: 1 208 263 5906
Email: airways@nidlink.com
URL: http://www.airwaysmag.com

Printed in Singapore

Designed by Scott Henderson, edited by John Wegg, and produced and typeset in 11 on 12pt Lydian by J.R. Taylor for SCOVAL Publishing Ltd

Acknowledgements

Special thanks to Boeing and to George Ditchfield from whose collection a large proportion of the photos in this book have been supplied. Where known, credit has been given but in certain instances, where the photographer was not known, please forgive me if due credit was not awarded.

The InCamera Series

This is the second in an exciting range of books which sets out to portray both civil and military aircraft, both from the early days of aviation to the present day. It covers what you (the aircraft enthusiast) have said you require — no demand — the highest standards of reproduction of some of the most beautiful photographs ever taken of aircraft, in black and white or full colour, and wherever possible in large plate reproduction.

Whether you are an avid modeller, connected with aviation, or just interested in the beauty and mystique of aircraft, this new series of books in the range 'INCAMERA' will bring to you breathtaking images of aircraft reproduced to the highest standards possible today.

Cover Picture

747-121 N747PA 'Jet Clipper America', the second 747 built, flies over the Cascade Mountains of Washington state on a test flight before delivery to Pan Am on 3 October 1970.

Boeing

Back Cover

Left: National Airlines took delivery of N77772, a 747-135 named 'Patricia', in September 1970. It served for six years and seven months with the Miami-based 'Sun King' airline before sale to Northwest Airlines in April 1976.

Boeing

Right: Known for its long association with the 747, Trans World Airlines has operated thirty-five 747s since the first 342-seat -131 was delivered on New Year's Eve 1969. Pictured is Fleet No 17103 (N93103) in the original 'double globe' colours. It was one of nine sold to the Iranian Air Force.

Boeing

The Boeing 747-100/200 InCamera

As the demand for air travel increased early in the 1960s, a series of events combined to give birth to the world's largest passenger airliner, an aircraft two and a half times the size of the Boeing 707. The idea that became the 747 actually started life as a strategic military airlifter. When the US Air Force selected Lockheed's C-5 over Boeing's proposal, the Seattle-based company went back to the drawing board to create a civil transport around the immensely powerful high-bypass turbofan engines that had been developed for the USAF's requirement.

After more than 200 ideas had been considered, the final design was the first wide-body, with a fuselage wide enough to accommodate two aisles and ten seats across, and an upper deck connected to the main cabin by a spiral staircase. It was a configuration inspired by the certainty that the 747 would be replaced by supersonic transports in ten years and be relegated to a freighter.

On 13 April 1966, Boeing announced the programme's launch with an order from Pan American for twenty-five aircraft. A new factory was built at Everett, north of Seattle, for the 747's final assembly. The prototype was rolled out on 30 September 1968 and made its first flight on 9 February 1969. A new age in air transport was on the horizon.

The first 747 delivery was made on 12 December 1969 to Pan Am, eighteen days before the type received certification by the Federal Aviation Administration. Service started — one day later than planned — on 22 January 1970. The hiccup was an indication of serious problems with the 747-100's Pratt & Whitney JT9D engines that saw a rash of engine changes and threatened the solvency of Boeing until solutions were devised. Eventually the troubles were overcome and the aircraft developed. The structurally strengthened 747-200B was introduced in 1970 to be built alongside the -100 series, until production of that model ended in 1976. The 747-200B was the first jetliner to be offered with engines from all three major manufacturers, the JT9D, plus the General Electric CF6 and Rolls-Royce RB211. It was also available in a Combi passenger/cargo version, with a Side Cargo Door (SCD); as a convertible passenger/freighter (the -200C with a hinged nose for cargo, and the option of a SCD); and as a pure-freighter (the -200F with SCD and/or nose door). A post-production modification was the SUD (Stretched Upper Deck) of the -300. The -200B was the most successful of the 747 variants until the -400 appeared, with a total of 393 built up to 1991, including seventy-eight Combis, thirteen -200Cs, seventy-three -200Fs, and four E-4s for the USAF. A total of 206 Pratt & Whitney-powered -100s were built, including 168 -100s, twenty-four 747SRs (Short Range), twelve -100Bs (similar to the SR), and two hybrid -100B SUDs. Two-digit (or a digit/letter combination) customer codes, for example 36 for BOAC/British Airways, are assigned by Boeing to complete an individual aircraft's designation (although these do not reflect the many engineering changes possible for each basic type).

Toward the end of the 1990s, many of the so-called -100/-200 'Classic' (that is, non-glass cockpit) 747s have changed ownership, sometimes many times, as they are replaced by more modern types. As 747-400s roll off the production line in the Pacific Northwest, many 747 Classics spend their final days in the aircraft boneyards of the Southwest before they are reduced to spares.

An icon of the late 20th century, the 747 has done more than any other aircraft to bring travel to the world, and thus help create a global economy and society. The awesome sight of a 747 taking off stills draws attention nearly thirty years on, and is likely to do so well into the next century.

This unique publication, 'Boeing 747-100/200 InCamera' captures most of the colour schemes applied to the early 747's many and varied operators over three decades.

The prototype 747 (appropriately registered N7470) in its original form. After initial certification was completed it was used in 747 development work, including air-to-air refuelling trials, and also engine testing for the 757 and 767 programmes. Between 1983 and 1986, the 'City of Everett' was stored at Las Vegas then used as a VC-25A mock-up. The Museum of Flight acquired the historic 747 in 1990 for its collection at Boeing Field.

Boeing

American Airlines, with a distinctive polished aluminium finish for its fleet, ordered sixteen 747-123 'Astroliners'. All were disposed of by 1984. This 1970-model, N9664, is now with United Airlines.

George Ditchfield Collection

Eighteen 747-136s were ordered by BOAC, thirteen of which were delivered in its golden 'Speedbird' colours. The other five arrived in the red-tailed union jack livery of British Airways, formed by the merger of BOAC and British European Airways in 1974. The eleventh -136, G-AWNK, is seen approaching London-Heathrow during 1973. Eight years later, it was sold to Trans World Airlines and today it is operational with Tower Air.

Scott Henderson

Another British Overseas Airways Corporation (BOAC) 747-136, this time G-AWNI, poses for the camera to emphasise its immense size.
Peter Keating

Throughout the early 1970s, it was not unusual to see a Boeing 747 carrying a spare engine to one of its stranded stablemates. Seen at Johannesburg, G-AWNG carries the 'fifth' pod. Delivered in 1972, this aircraft is still with British Airways although — along with the rest of BA's -100 fleet — its retirement is fast approaching.
Peter Keating

During the transition period from BOAC to British Airways, most of the 747 fleet carried the new BA titles on the old BOAC colours, as demonstrated by G-AWNE, seen here at London-Heathrow in 1974.
Author's Collection

It was not until April 1976 that Pakistan International Airways acquired their first 747s from TAP. Both -282B aircraft (AP-AYW is illustrated) are still with PIA.

George Ditchfield

PIA's AP-BCM is a 747-217B, one of four aircraft with JT9Ds purchased from CP Air (now Canadian Airlines International). It is seen at Manchester in March 1993 wearing the airline's latest colours.

George Ditchfield

Philippine Airlines has operated several 747-200Bs since January 1980, when they went onto the Manila — Honolulu — San Francisco route. Delivered in February that year, N742PR — one of the original four CF6-powered 747-2F6Bs — approaches Zürich in March 1984.

Scotpic

This time sporting the new image of Philippine Airlines, N742PR is seen at Manchester in 1988. PAL entered receivership in June 1998 and four months later shut down operations. The beleaguered airline has since restarted limited domestic services and is hoping to resume some international routes.

George Ditchfield

Boeing 747-211B G-NIGB, built for Wardair, is towed across the ramp at Manchester in April 1988. The aircraft served only one year with British Caledonian Airways before it was merged into British Airways. Subsequently, the aircraft was sold.

George Ditchfield

After BCal was acquired by British Airways in 1988, some 747s appeared with the new Caledonian Airways identity. One such example was ex-SAS -283B G-BMGS 'Loch Ness', leased from BA and seen at Manchester in August 1989. It later became Virgin Atlantic Airways's 'Shady Lady'.

George Ditchfield

Starting in 1985, Air Pacific, the colourful airline of Fiji, has operated a number of leased 747-200Bs, mostly from QANTAS and Air New Zealand. With the exception of the recently applied 'Fiji' on the tail, the livery has been unchanged. Leased in July 1993 for three years, ZK-NZY has since been replaced with a Fijian-registered example, again leased from the Australian flag carrier.

Scotpic

Delta Air Lines's association with the 747-100 was fairly short-lived. All five of their -132s were delivered between September 1970 and November 1971. The first aircraft was returned to Boeing in September 1974 and, within three years, the remainder of the fleet had followed suit. This classic shot of N9896, Delta's first aircraft, was taken just before delivery.

Boeing

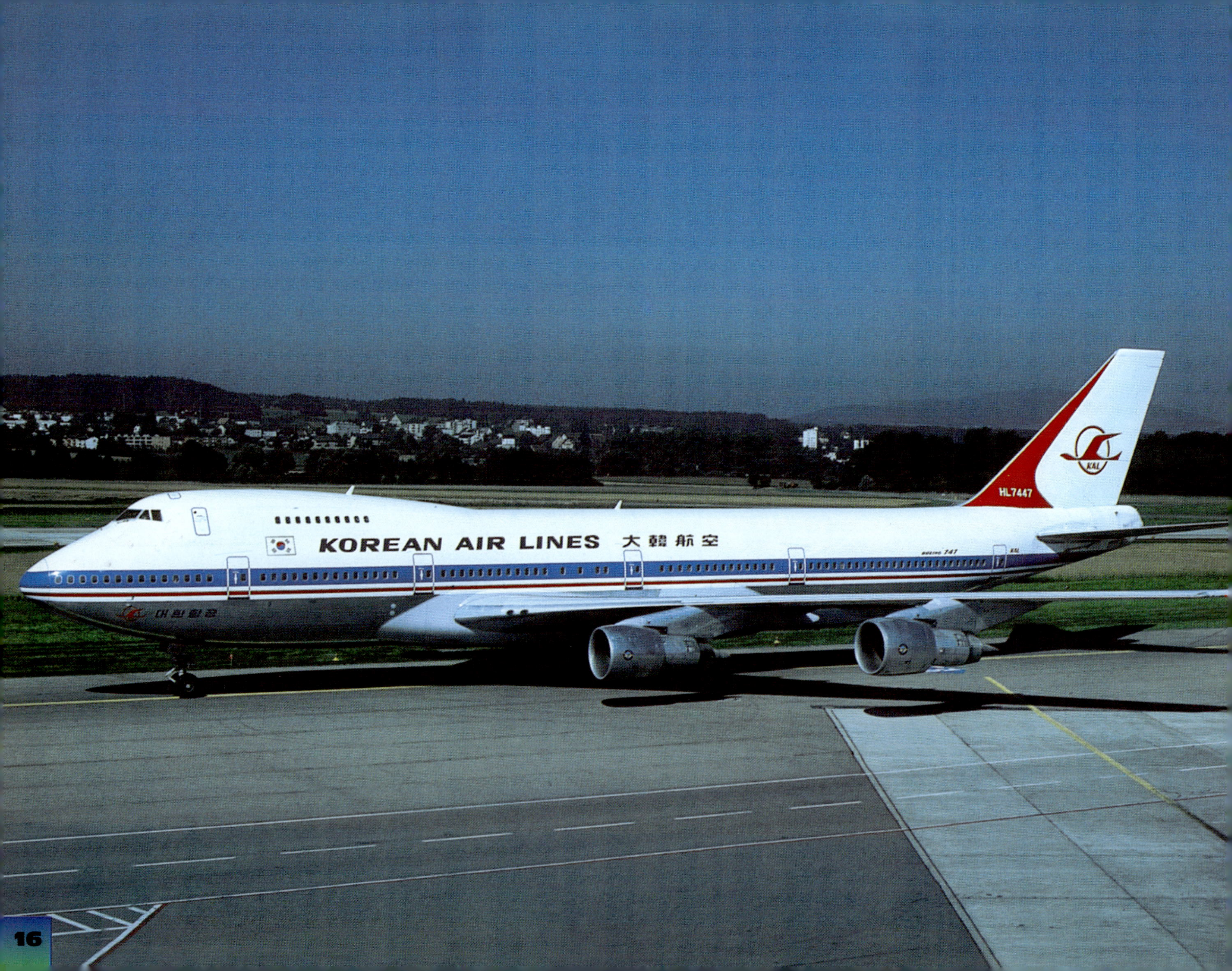
KOREAN AIR LINES 大韓航空
대한항공
HL7447
KAL
BOEING 747

Left: Korean Air Lines (now Korean Air) has operated many 747s since 1973. This aircraft, HL7447, an ex-Condor 747-230B, seen here in an earlier livery, was leased for twelve years from June 1979. Korean sub-leased it for short periods to both Saudia and Nigeria Airways.
George Ditchfield

Top right: Because of South Korea's industrial expansion late in the 1970s, Korean Air Lines invested heavily in 747 freighters. This -2B5F (HL7451) was the first to join its fleet in 1980 and has worn three different liveries. In March 1994, it was still in a polished aluminium finish.
Author's Collection

Lower right: After the infamous shootdown of flight KAL007 by the Soviet Union in 1983, the airline changed its image as illustrated by HL7458. This -2B5B originally served as an all-passenger aircraft before being converted to a freighter for Korean Air Cargo.
George Ditchfield Collection

17

Cathay Pacific Airways first introduced the 747-200B in 1980 as a replacement for 707s and to supplement its TriStars on Asian routes. In December 1984, in its original green and white trim, VR-HIH, a 747-267B with RB211 engines, taxies by the skyline of Hong Kong.

Arthur J Payne

During the 1980s, Cathay Pacific converted a number of its 747-200Bs to freighters. One of these was VR-HIH, which served long enough to be painted into the company's latest corporate image. Pictured at London-Gatwick in November 1996, it also carries the airline's 50th anniversary logo.

Mike Axe

In March 1970, Air France took delivery of their first of sixteen 747-128s. Like its European neighbours Lufthansa and British Airways, it has subsequently acquired later models. At Paris-Orly in September 1972 in its original colours, F-BPVH passes a 707 predecessor. This 747 was eventually sold for parts in the US and scrapped at Opa-locka, Florida, in March 1997.

Dean Slaybaugh

A few of the Air France 747-128s served well into the 1990s, such as F-BPVJ — the 200th 747 off the line — which was delivered in 1973. Until 1982, it was registered in the US as N28903.

George Ditchfield Collection

The unmistakable and attractive colours of Iraqi Airways, seen here on YI-AGN, were once a familiar sight at the major airports of Europe, and at Tokyo, Bangkok, and Rio de Janeiro. The airline still has its three JT9D-powered 747-270Cs, all grounded since the Gulf War in 1991.

Boeing

This 747-1D1 started life in 1971 as a -124 with Continental Airlines, named after the company's founder, Robert F. Six. Sold to Wardair of Canada in 1974, it eventually passed to a leasing company and served with a number of airlines, including as TF-ABS with Air Atlanta of Iceland, which operated it on behalf of Saudia. It is seen here in pristine condition, taxiing at Manchester, although it has since been retired and broken up for spares.

George Ditchfield

One of the original two -282Bs delivered in 1972 to Transportes Aereos Portugueses (TAP), CS-TJB 'Brasil' is caught during a night turnaround at Düsseldorf in October 1976. The aircraft was sold to TWA in 1984 and is currently operated by Tower Air.

Michael Hovel via George Ditchfield Collection

Bought from KLM Royal Dutch Airlines on 25 October 1989, America West used 747-206B N531AW for only 22 months before it was returned to its lessor and parked at Las Vegas. The aircraft was broken up at Kingman, Arizona, in 1996.

George Ditchfield Collection

26

Left: Royal Jordanian Airlines (Alia) 747-2D3B Combi JY-AFA 'Prince Ali' is seen on a test flight in March 1977. Alia had three CF6-powered 747s which were operated for eleven years. They were regular visitors to Western Europe and, on occasions, were flown by His Majesty King Hussein of Jordan, an accomplished pilot.
Boeing

Top right: Alia changed its colours early in the 1980s. Here, JY-AFA displays its exceptionally smart finish, featuring a large gold crown on the tail.
George Ditchfield

Lower right: New image, same aircraft: JY-AFA is seen at London-Heathrow in April 1987. Two years later, it was acquired by UTA (Union de Transports Aériens). The airline's other two -2D3Bs went to British Caledonian Airways.
George Ditchfield Collection

27

Since their acquisition in 1975, Middle East Airlines's three 747-2B4B Combis have spent more than half their lives on lease to other airlines because of the civil unrest in Lebanon. In its original colour scheme, OD-AGH is seen on a pre-delivery test flight in May 1975.

Boeing

Alias OD-AGI, N203AE poses for the camera at Manchester on a sunny afternoon during December 1991, showing off its modified colours. Over the past twenty years, Saudia, Gulf Air, British Airways, Garuda, and Philippine Airlines have all had their paintwork applied to this aircraft.

George Ditchfield

This time caught at London-Gatwick, N203AE wears the latest simplified version of MEA colours, applied after its lease to Philippine Airlines. Over the years, the look of MEA may have changed but the cedar jet logo, a national symbol of Lebanon, has been retained.

Mike Axe

The Spanish flag carrier Iberia acquired its first two 747-156s in 1970 for trans-Atlantic services from Madrid. Two years later, 747-256Bs were introduced: EC-EEK 'Garcia Lorca' is a Combi version seen on approach to Madrid-Barajas in July 1991.

Scott Henderson

A 747-283B Combi, formerly with SAS as 'Knut Viking', SE-DFZ is another machine that has had several paint schemes applied during its many leases. Foxtrot Zulu arrived at Stockholm in 1979 and after four years Scandinavian service was leased to Nigeria Airways for a year. The aircraft is depicted at London-Heathrow in June 1983, operating the airline's flag route from Lagos.

George Ditchfield Collection

ALITALIA was an early European customer for the 747. In 1970, it took delivery of two 365-seat 747-143s, including I-DEMA which was named after the first man on the moon, Neil Alden Armstrong. After eleven years of service in ALITALIA's distinctive livery, it was sold back to Boeing.

Scotpic

This 747-130 was delivered new in May 1970 to Lufthansa, which flew it for more than eight years. It was acquired by Aer Lingus in January 1979 as EI-BED and often leased to other airlines. Twice it was used by LAN Chile for three-month periods, and it is seen here at New York-JFK in January 1989 during the occasion of the first lease.

Author's Collection

Delivered to the national carrier of the island of Madagascar in January 1979, -2B2B Combi 5R-MFT has been the sole 747 in the airline's fleet for the past nineteen years and is used primarily on flights between Antananarivo and Paris.

George Ditchfield Collection

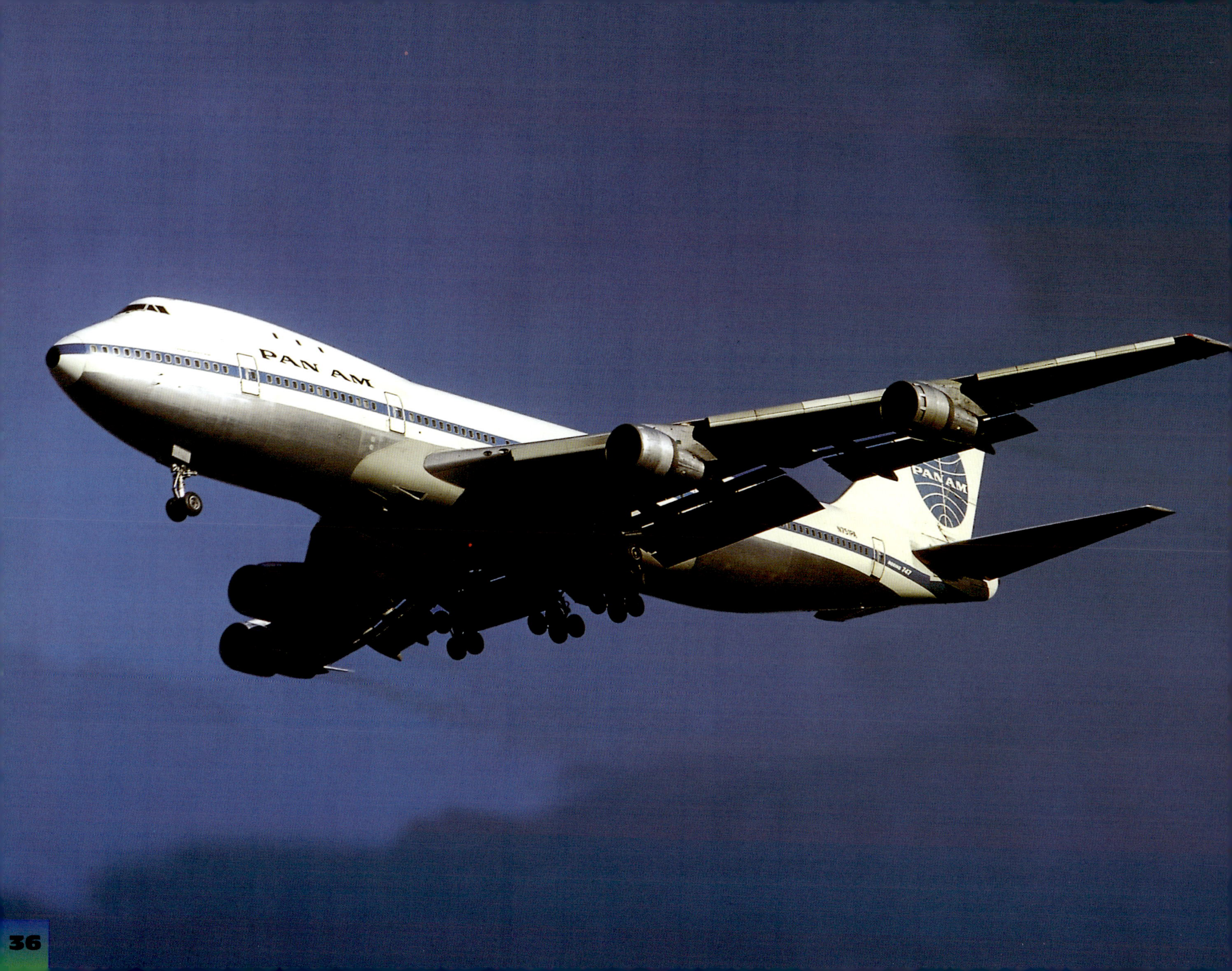
PAN AM
PAN AM

Left: Arguably the most famous name in the airline industry, Pan American World Airways was the launch customer for the 747. This is the 33rd 747 off the line, -121 N751PA 'Clipper Midnight Sun', which was delivered in April 1970. After eighteen years in Pan Am service, the aircraft was sold to rival TWA and eventually surrendered to the breakers torch in Arizona.
Scott Henderson

Top right: Caught on approach to London-Heathrow, N750PA 'Clipper Rambler' wears a later style of airline titles. It spent its entire life with Pan Am and was eventually scrapped at Marana, Arizona.
Author's Collection

Lower right: In 1980, most PA 747s changed names to those relating to the high seas. Formerly 'Clipper Red Jacket', 'Clipper Ocean Herald' (N737PA) taxies at Manchester in March 1986 wearing the final Pan Am colour scheme.
George Ditchfield

Braniff International Airways, well-known for its colourful paint schemes, operated several 747-200Bs up to the time operations ceased in May 1982. All were painted orange — hence the 'Big Orange' moniker — as seen on 747-227B N605BN. This aircraft was never delivered to Braniff and eventually ended up with Northwest.

Boeing

An airline easily recognised by the Star of David on its tail, El Al has used 747s since June 1971. This is a -258C freighter, 4X-AXF, seen on approach to Athens in February 1979.

Author's Collection

The prestigious CF6-powered Boeing 747-2G4B 29000 is known by the US Air Force as a VC-25A. When the President of the United States is on board, such as during this visit to London-Heathrow in June 1997, the aircraft's radio call-sign is 'Air Force One'. The two presidential 747s are undoubtedly the most filmed in the world.

Author's Collection

One of MEA's 747-2B4B Combis, N203AE, is seen on one of its many leases. Gulf Air used the aircraft from March 1984 to October 1985 and it is seen here on the maintenance ramp of British Airways at London-Heathrow.

Peter Keating

A familiar sight at major European airports is a 747 of Air Canada. One of the original four -133s delivered to the airline, C-FTOB is seen at the point of lift-off for another North Atlantic crossing.

Author's Collection

In December 1993, Air Canada changed its image and adopted a dark blue tail and large red titles, although the famous maple leaf insignia was retained. The new colours are displayed in June 1994 by C-FTOC, a 747-133 delivered in 1971.

P J Cooper

The prominent shamrock emblem of Aer Lingus has been carried on the tail of a 747 since 1970. The first of two 366-seat -148s delivered to the airline was EI-ASI 'Padraig/St. Patrick', which served on the North Atlantic until 1994, when it was sold to Kabo Air of Nigeria.

Boeing

Martinair Holland bought two CF6-powered 747-21ACs which traditionally have been used for cargo operations during the northern winter and passenger work in summer. The original example, PH-MCE 'Prins van Oranje' delivered in 1987, is seen landing at Málaga in June 1997, operating a holiday charter from Amsterdam.

Scott Henderson

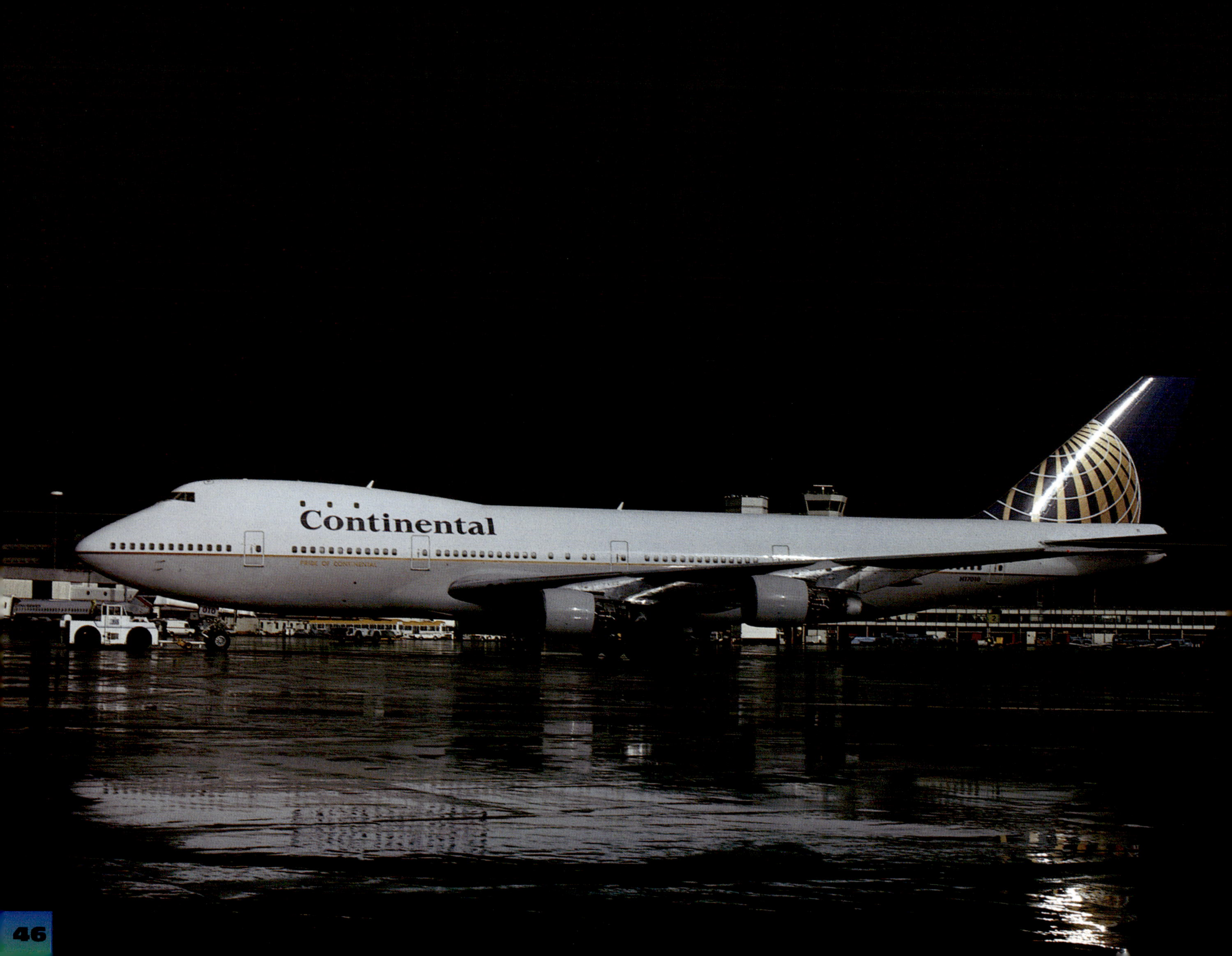
Continental

Left: Continental Airlines purchased four 747-124s in 1970 but these 'Proud Birds of the Pacific' were returned to Boeing four years later during the so-called fuel crisis. In 1987, Continental's parent, Texas Air, acquired PEOPLExpress and thus CO inherited several early 747s, some of which are still in service with Guam-based Continental Micronesia. This ex-ALITALIA 747-143, N17010, operated in Continental colours from 1987 to 1995, until its sale to TWA.

George Ditchfield

Top right: On approach to Los Angeles in June 1990, N603PE wears Continental's 'Golden Jet' colours. Two years later, a change was made to a white fuselage and blue and gold tail logo.

Scott Henderson

Lower right: Following Continental's takeover of PEOPLExpress, several of the latter's 747s appeared in a transitional livery, combining PE colours with CO titles.

George Ditchfield Collection

47

Royal Air Maroc is unusual because it has operated only one each of the 747-200, -400, and SP (Special Performance) models. The JT9D-powered 747-2B6B Combi (CN-RME) was delivered to RAM in September 1978 and has spent most of its life operating from Casablanca to Paris, Jeddah, Montréal, and New York.

George Ditchfield

Minerve, a French independent airline, leased an ex-SAS 747-283B in 1987 for inclusive tour charters, mainly to Réunion and the French West Indies. The company merged with AOM French Airlines on 1 January 1992 and shortly after F-GHBM was retired. Eventually, it was broken up at San Antonio, Texas. Here the aircraft is seen in happier days in February 1988 at Paris-Orly.

George Ditchfield Collection

Cameroon Airlines took delivery of its sole 747-2H7B Combi, TJ-CAB 'Mont Cameroon', in February 1981. The aircraft, used mainly on routes from Douala to Johannesburg and Paris, demonstrates one of the more attractive schemes from West Africa.

Author's Collection

The exotic colours of the sole 747 in Air Gabon's fleet are displayed by this 1978-model -2Q2B Combi, while on a test flight over Washington state before delivery to Libreville. Although registered TR-LXK, the aircraft has never operated as such, instead temporarily using N1248E and then F-ODJG.

Boeing

Posing in its original colours is 9K-ADA, the first of four 747-269B Combis for Kuwait Airways, Boeing's 50th 747 customer. After delivery to the airline in July 1978, the aircraft was a regular sight at European airports until it was sold in 1995 to American International Airways.

After the 1991 Gulf War, Kuwait Airways modified its colours as modelled by 9K-ADD. The aircraft, a 747-269B Combi, joined the fleet in 1982 and, after sixteen years, is still active.

George Ditchfield

After three years and nine months with American Airlines, 747-123 N9668 was bought by NASA (National Aeronautics & Space Administration) and converted to a carrier for the Space Shuttle's Orbiter. Re-registered as N905NA, until October 1988 — when a second aircraft was acquired by NASA — it was the sole Orbiter transporter.

C T Robbins

National Airlines took delivery of N77772, a 747-135 named 'Patricia', in September 1970. It served for six years and seven months with the Miami-based 'Sun King' airline before sale to Northwest Airlines in April 1976.

Boeing

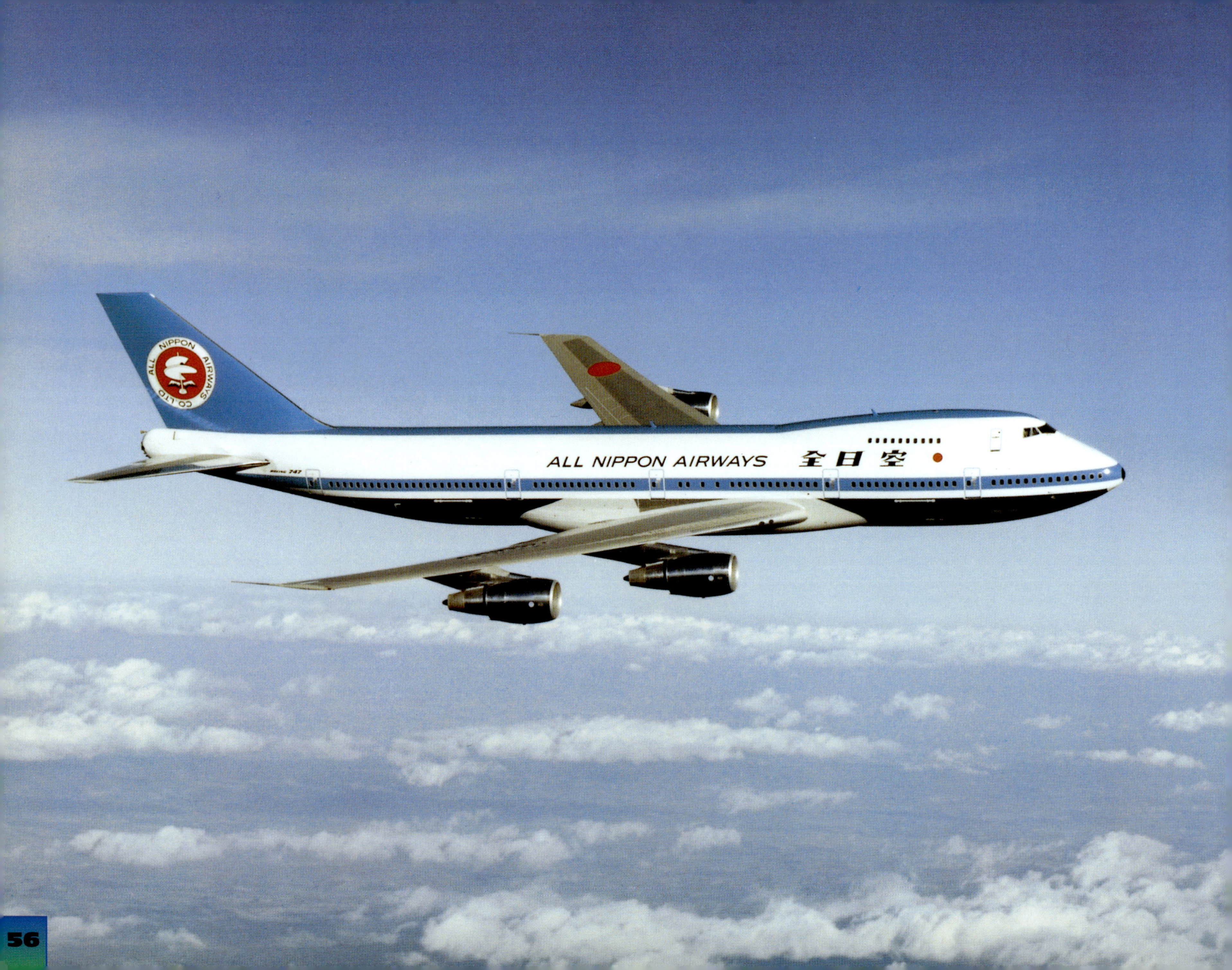
ALL NIPPON AIRWAYS
全日空
ALL NIPPON AIRWAYS CO. LTD
747

Left: The fourth of seventeen 747SR-81s built for All Nippon Airways, JA8136 dips a wing for the Boeing camera ship. ANA's 747s were the first to have seats for 500 passengers and currently accommodate 528 in a two-class layout.
Boeing

Top right: During the mid-1980s, All Nippon adopted a new image as seen on JA8175, a 747-281B used for international service. Only five examples are now in service with ANA, and they are confined to intra-Asian routes.
George Ditchfield Collection

Lower right: Nippon Cargo Airlines was established in 1978 as an all-cargo subsidiary of ANA. Its first two -281Fs entered service in May 1985, on the Tokyo (Narita) — San Francisco — New York route. NCA now operates seven 747-200Fs, including JA8191, a 1990-model, plus one converted 747SR-81.
George Ditchfield Collection

57

Air Afrique's sole 747-2S4F shows off the multi-national carrier's attractive livery. Named 'Lomé', TU-TAP was delivered in 1980 and flew for the Abidjan-based consortium for only four years. It has since operated for Korean Air Cargo as HL7474.

Boeing

Wardair, the pioneering Canadian charter operator, in 1974 bought Continental's 747-100 N26864 and re-registered it C-FFUN. 'Romeo Vachon', named after a pioneer bush pilot, was a frequent visitor to the UK and is seen here at Manchester in 1982, taxiing out for another trans-Atlantic crossing.

George Ditchfield

Although VIASA of Venezuela never ordered a 747, it leased several aircraft, the first from KLM. This -273C (N749WA) was leased from World Airways from June 1981 to October 1983 to operate scheduled cargo service from Caracas to Miami and New York.

Author's Collection

Trans International Airlines bought Saturn Airways, another 'non-sked', in 1979, and then changed its name from TIA to Transamerica Airlines. At the same time, it took delivery of N741TV, the first of five 747-271Cs with CF6 engines. The 488-seat aircraft supplemented DC-8s on trans-Atlantic and trans-Pacific civilian and military charters, and also flew some scheduled services.

Author's Collection

The unmistakable flying kangaroo of QANTAS has adorned 747s since September 1971. Boeing 747-238B VH-EBF 'City of Adelaide' is seen setting off from London-Heathrow for a 22-hour trip to Sydney, wearing the colours used on the fleet from 1971 to 1984.

Scott Henderson

Although the majority of QANTAS's twenty-two 747-238Bs have been replaced by -438s, VH-EBA 'City of Canberra' survived long enough in the fleet to carry the airline's latest colours, demonstrated to good effect in this dramatic shot taken on a rare sunny day at Manchester.

George Ditchfield

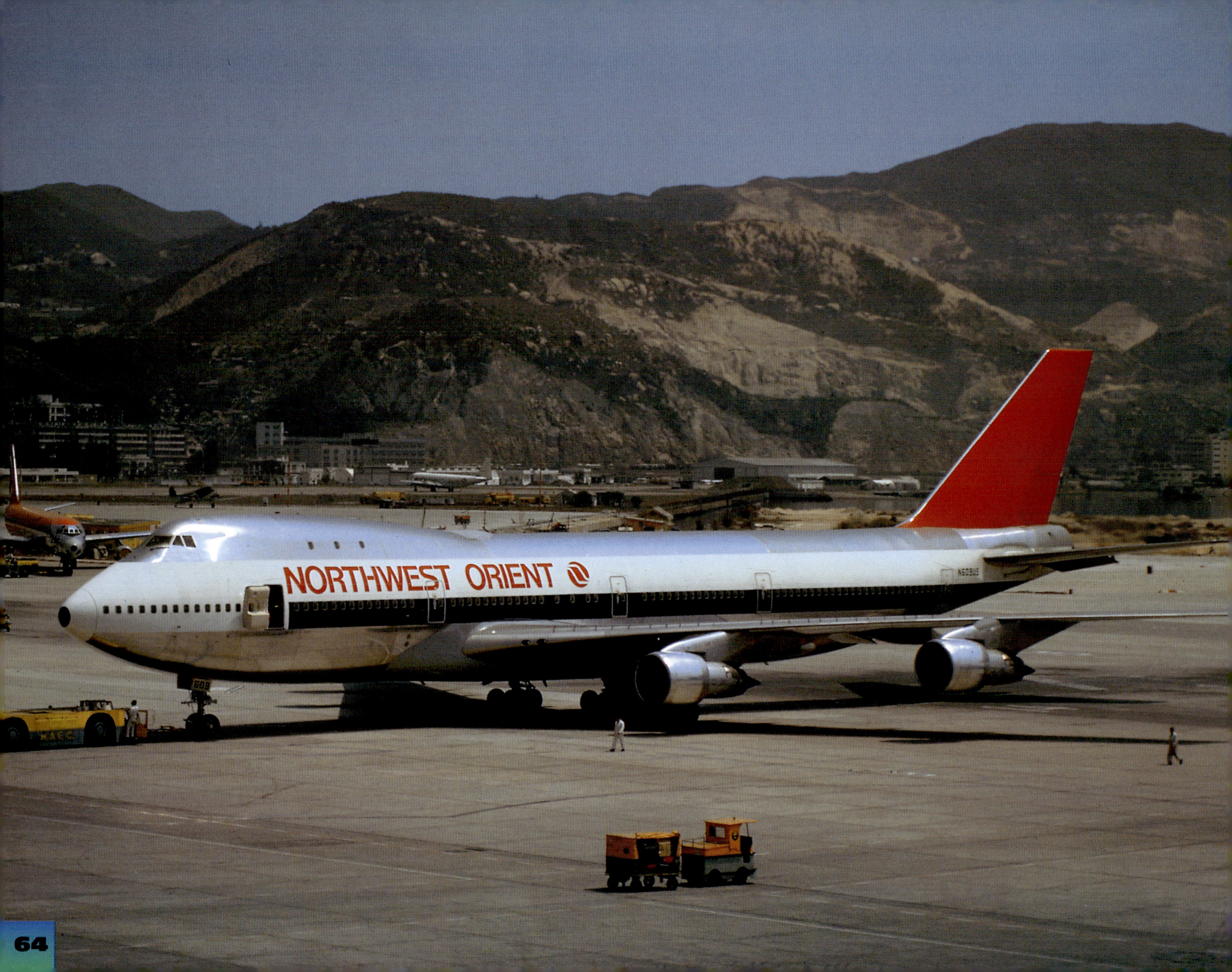
NORTHWEST ORIENT

Left: Longtime 747 operator Northwest Airlines introduced 747-151s into service in 1970 on its trans-Pacific routes. Wearing the early colour scheme of natural metal, white, and blue fuselage, with the company's trademark red tail, N609US is towed across the ramp at Hong Kong's Kai Tak International Airport on 21 March 1971.
Scotpic

Top right: During 1986, Northwest dropped the word 'Orient' from its marketing name to emphasise its image as an international airline rather than one restricted to the Pacific Rim. In this fine portrait, 747-151 N602US approaches Tokyo-Narita in November 1988. This veteran (the second 747 to be delivered to NW) was sold in 1995 for spares.
George Ditchfield Collection

Lower right: Northwest again changed its livery in 1994 with a new red top and grey fuselage finish, as seen on 747-251B N627US on approach to Narita.
Y Kurimoto via George Ditchfield Collection

Seaboard World Airlines, formerly Seaboard & Western, was the first all-cargo airline to operate a 747-200F. Called 'Containerships' by the airline, the first of six -245Fs was N701SW, seen here on a pre-delivery test flight. SWA was acquired by Flying Tigers in 1980, which took delivery of the last two -245Fs.

Boeing

CP Air operated four 747-217Bs in its stunning orange and red livery, both on scheduled trans-Pacific and trans-Atlantic routes, and on charters. Seen here at Manchester in April 1982 is C-FCRB 'Empress of Canada' about to depart on a charter to its homeland. All four 747s were sold to PIA and replaced by DC-10-30s.

George Ditchfield

One short-lived US operator of the 747 was Eastern Air Lines. It ordered four aircraft but the delivery positions were sold to TWA and instead it leased three Pan Am 747-121s for fifteen months. Eastern planned to acquire two 747-238Bs from QANTAS, including N372EA (ex VH-EBC) seen here at Sydney-Kingsford Smith in March 1980, for Miami — London service, but the route was awarded to Pan Am and the sale was not concluded.

Author's Collection

First delivered as a 747-1D1 to Wardair in April 1973, C-FDJC was operated by Nationair from December 1989 to May 1993, with several short leases to Garuda and Saudia for Hajj work. The aircraft is seen at Manchester in September 1991.

George Ditchfield

From 1973, Olympic Airways, the flag carrier of Greece, operated two 747-284Bs on its Athens — New York route. In 1985, one of the original aircraft was sold to TWA and three -212Bs were acquired from Singapore Airlines to expand service to Asia, Australia, Canada, and South Africa. One of these, SX-OAE 'Olympic Peace', is seen on approach to Sydney.

Author's Collection

All of the main deck windows of Air-India's 747 fleet feature a red Rajasthani-style arch surround to help promote the type as the airline's 'Palace in the Sky'. One of eleven 747-237Bs delivered, VT-EFU 'Krishna Deva Raya' displays this unique livery while taxiing at Hong Kong-Kai Tak in April 1986.

Arthur J Payne

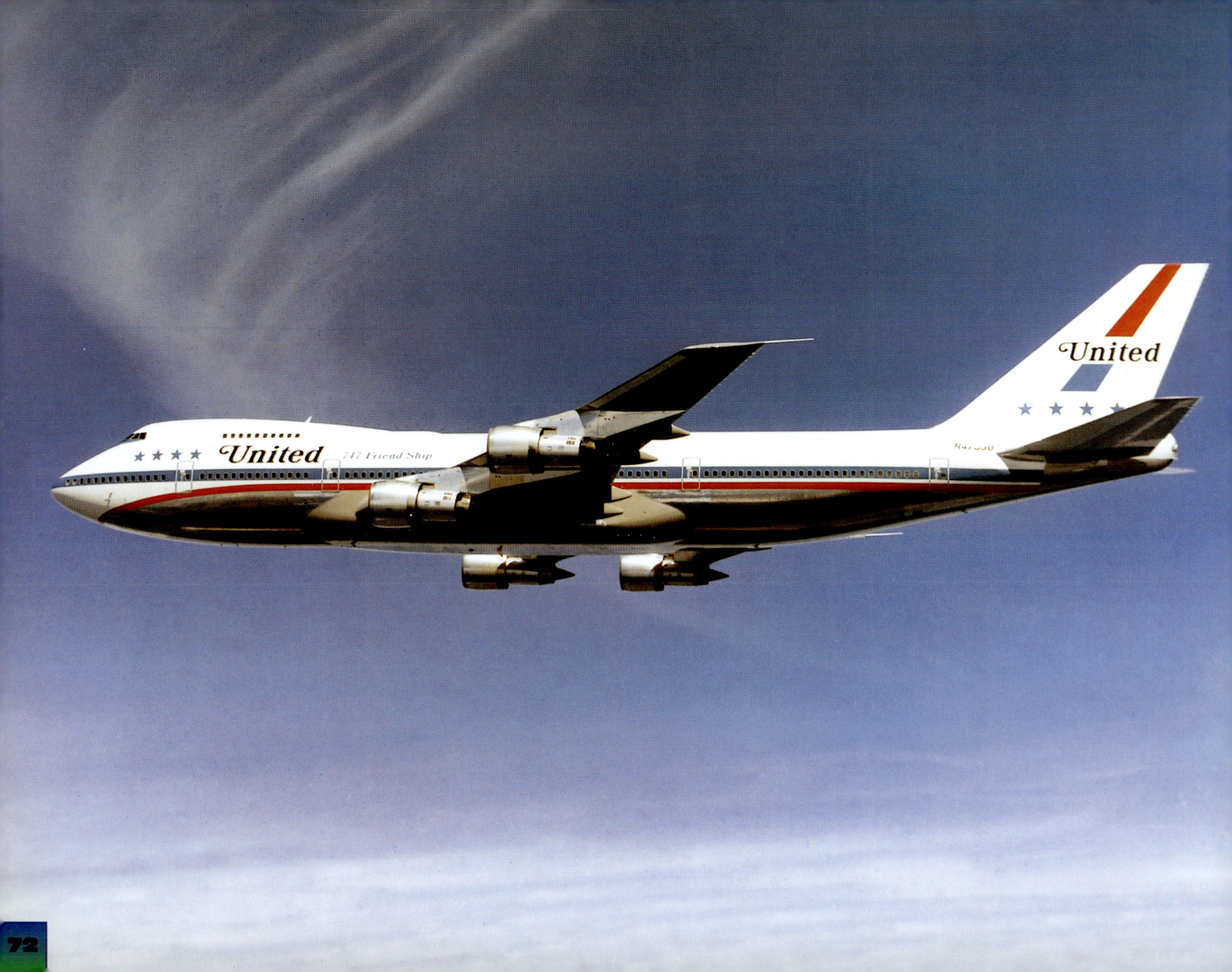
United
747 Friend Ship
United

Left: Until its takeover of Pan Am's Pacific network in 1986, United Airlines 747s were rarely seen outside of the US. This is one of its fleet of 747-122s, N4735U, wearing the 'Four Star Friend Ship' titles which were introduced in 1973 on a play of the airline's longtime slogan, 'fly the friendly skies'.
Boeing

Top right: On approach to Los Angeles in July 1992, N152UA, one of only two 747-222Bs, displays the attractive red, orange, and blue colours that United adopted in 1974 and retained for two decades.
Scott Henderson

Lower right: In January 1993, United unveiled a 'Worldwide Service' image of dark grey, blue, and red. Ex-QANTAS 747-238B N159UA, on approach to Osaka in May 1993, displays the distinctive colours.
George Ditchfield Collection

73

The last 747-230B delivered to Lufthansa, in February 1987, D-ABZH 'Bonn' displays the conservative 'flying crane' colours worn by the German flag carrier's fleet from 1968.

George Ditchfield

In 1988, Lufthansa modified its colour scheme by dispensing with the fuselage cheat line and adopting a white and grey fuselage. Named 'Köln', D-ABYX is one of the airline's CF6-powered -230B Combis, several of which have now been converted to freighters.

George Ditchfield Collection

Highland Express Airways started a low-fare service in July 1987 to Newark from London (Stansted), Birmingham, and Prestwick with a 499-seat ex-American Airlines 747-123. The airline lasted only a few months and was wound up by the end of the year. Named 'The Highlander', G-HIHO is seen on take-off from London-Gatwick.

Author's Collection

Flying Tigers ordered four JT9D-powered 747-249Fs in 1978 which were delivered from October 1979 for its trans-Pacific routes. With its acquisition of Seaboard World, FTL acquired six more -200Fs and increased its 747 freighter fleet with second-hand purchases and various leases. The company was taken over by Federal Express in 1989, the year that this original -249F (N807FT) crashed on approach to Kuala Lumpur.

Arthur J Payne

THAI International has operated the 747-200B since 1979. Over the last few years, the fleet has been replaced by the -300 and -400 series and the last two -2D7Bs were sold in 1997 for conversion to freighters. Here, HS-TGG 'Sriwanna', the penultimate survivor, is caught preparing to land at Frankfurt in May 1983.

For three and half years in the 1970s, Air Siam was Thailand's second international airline, operating a sole 747 on the Bangkok — Hong Kong — Tokyo — Honolulu route. The first aircraft used was a -148 leased from Aer Lingus as HS-VGB 'Doi Suthep', seen here at Hong Kong in 1975. It was replaced in April 1976 with HS-VGG, a -206B leased from KLM.

Author's Collection

Singapore Airlines has been a major customer for the 747 since its first order for 747-212Bs in 1972, some of which were delivered as 'Super Bs' with improved JT9D engines. These nineteen aircraft have now been replaced by -300 'Big Tops' and -400 'Megatops'. Captured on approach to Osaka in November 1981 is 9V-SQO, a Super B which displays the airline's regal blue and yellow livery.

George Ditchfield Collection

One 747-212F, 9V-SKQ seen here at London-Heathrow in the revised Singapore colours of gold and dark blue, was delivered new in 1988. Today, Singapore cargo moves by 747-412F 'Mega Arks'.

Author's Collection

VARIG of Brazil took delivery of three 747-2L5B Combi aircraft in 1981 which had been built for Libyan Arab Airlines but whose sale was blocked by US government sanctions. They were later replaced by -341s. Illustrated is 747-244B PP-VNW which VARIG leased in 1987 from South African Airways.

Author's Collection

Aerolíneas Argentinas did not start 747 operations until January 1977, with the first of seven JT9D-powered 747-287Bs. Six of the seven are still in service. The initial aircraft, LV-LZD, eventually became the 'Maiden Voyager' of the Virgin Atlantic Airways fleet.

Boeing

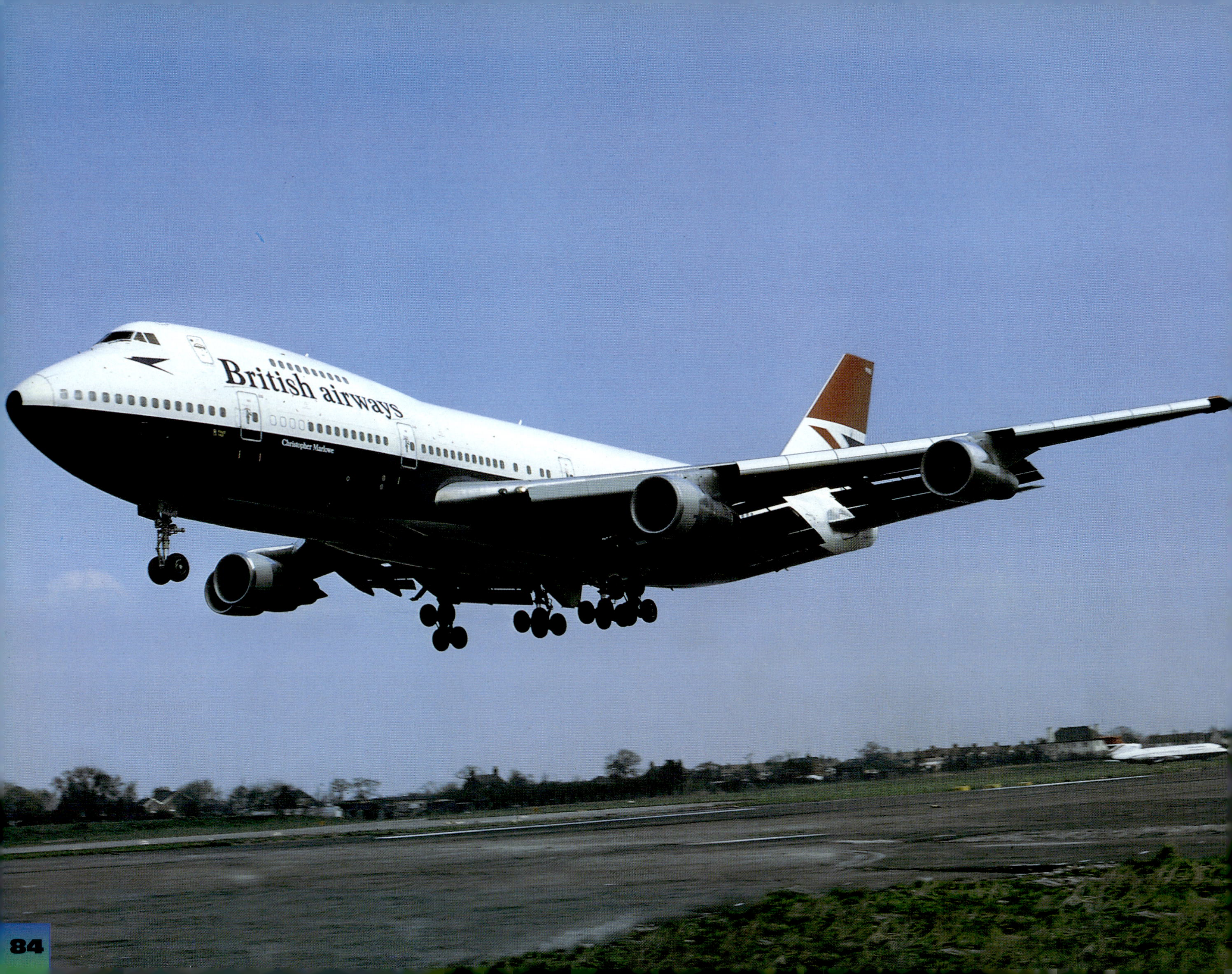
British airways
Christopher Marlowe

Left: British Airways has operated a total of forty-four 747-100s and -200Bs since 1970. In this 'Classic' shot, one of the original -136s, G-AWND 'Christopher Marlow', is preparing to land at Manchester in April 1980. November Delta was unfortunate to be on the ground in Kuwait in August 1990 when Iraqi forces invaded the country and it was destroyed in February 1991.

George Ditchfield

Top right: In 1980, BA deleted 'Airways' from its aircraft and publicity material. However, it soon discovered that the change was unpopular with the travelling public and within two years had restored the full titles. Here we see 747-136 G-AWNC on approach to London-Heathrow in August 1981 sporting the short-lived livery.

Peter Keating

Lower right: Another change to the BA identity occurred at the end of 1984, when a patriotic tail fin design was adopted incorporating the BA coat-of-arms on a field of royal blue. An RB211-powered 747-236B, G-BDXF 'City of York', displays these colours at Manchester in March 1990.

George Ditchfield

Founded in 1961 as a charter subsidiary of Lufthansa, Condor Flugdienst was the first non-scheduled operator of a 747. Its first aircraft, D-ABYF, was delivered in May 1971 in a 470-seat layout (the first 747 with a ten-abreast configuration) and was used initially for flights to Spanish holiday resorts.

AVIANCA of Colombia, one of the oldest airlines in the world, introduced an ex-Continental Airlines 747-124 in December 1976 on routes from Bogotá to Miami, New York, San Juan, Madrid, Paris, and Frankfurt. Seen above, this 747-259B Combi, HK-2980X 'Cartagena de Indias', spent sixteen years with the airline.

George Ditchfield

Air Lanka, the national carrier of Sri Lanka (formerly Ceylon), leased two 747-238Bs from QANTAS in 1984, including 4R-ULF 'King Vijaya'. They were used for flights to Europe and the Far East but the type proved to be unsuitable for the small airline and both were returned three years later.

Author's Collection

Corsair was established in 1981 as Corse-Air International to operate holiday charters between France and Mediterranean sunspots. In June 1991, the first of six 747s was acquired. A former Pan Am -121 is seen here at Manchester in April 1994.

George Ditchfield

PEOPLExpress, a low-fares, no-frills carrier, was a child of US deregulation. It operated a total of nine 490-seat 747-100/-200Bs between 1983 and 1987, when the airline was merged into Continental Airlines. An ex-QANTAS 747-238B, N607PE displays the carrier's striking colours at London-Gatwick in 1985.

Author's Collection

Since 1971, KLM has operated seventeen 747-206Bs, ten of which have been CF6-powered Combi versions. During the 1980s, several of these were converted with a Stretched Upper Deck, including PH-BUL 'Charles A. Lindbergh', seen here at Amsterdam-Schiphol in February 1979, three months after delivery.

Scott Henderson

Air Hong Kong was formed in 1986 under the umbrella of the Swire Group, which also owns Cathay Pacific Airways, to operate cargo services with Boeing 707s. Several 747s were added from 1991, including VR-HKO, an ex-Federal Express/Flying Tigers -249F, delivered in March 1994.

George Ditchfield

In 1996, Air Hong Kong acquired three newer 747-2L5B freighters (aircraft built for Libyan Arab) from Cathay Pacific Airways to replace its original examples. At the same time, a new livery was adopted as depicted by VR-HME, seen at Manchester in July 1996.

George Ditchfield

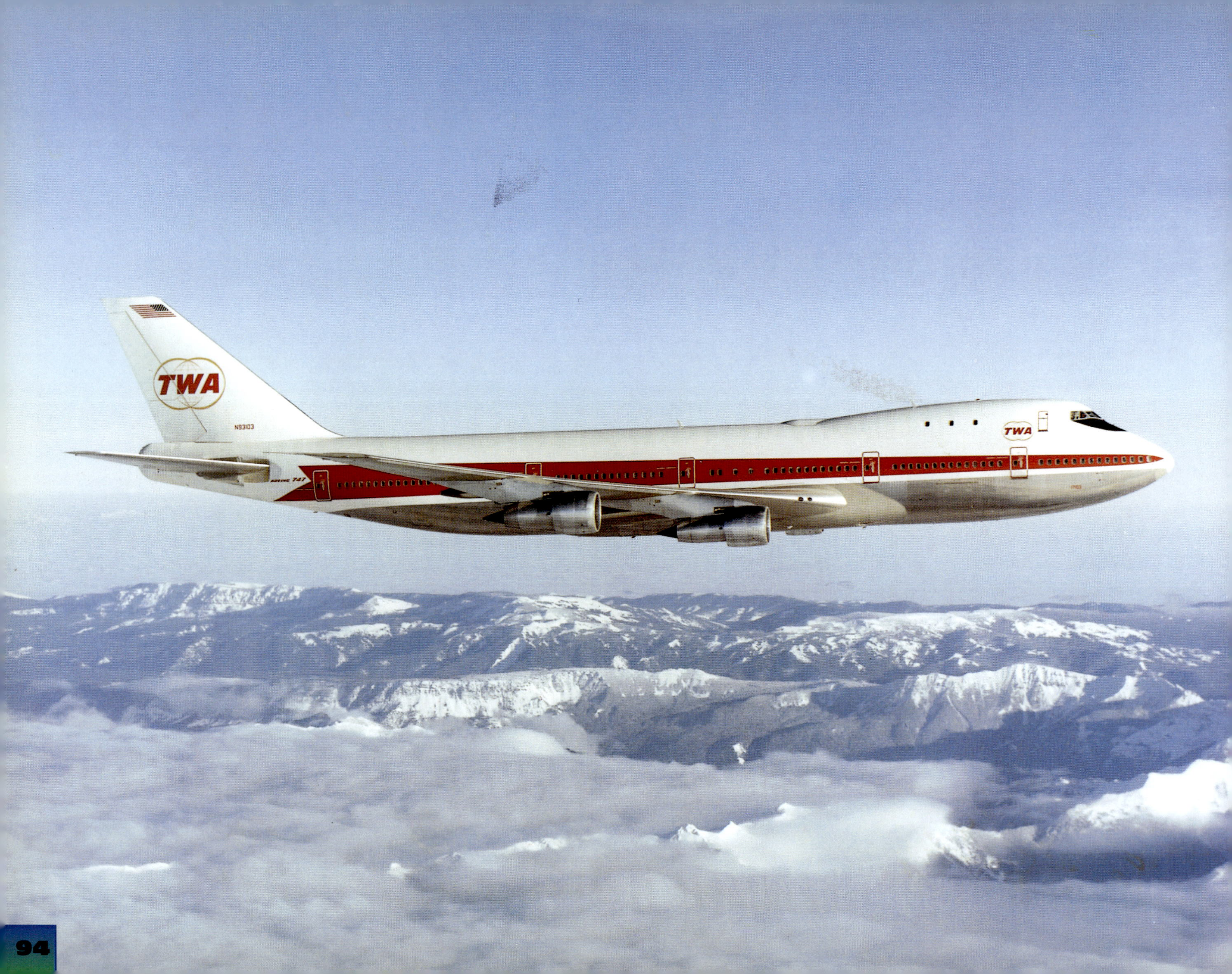
TWA
N93103
TWA

Left: Known for its long association with the 747, Trans World Airlines has operated thirty-five 747s since the first 342-seat -131 was delivered on New Year's Eve 1969. Pictured is Fleet No 17103 (N93103) in the original 'double globe' colours. It was one of nine sold to the Iranian Air Force.

Boeing

Top right: Originally delivered to TWA in March 1970, 747-131 N93105 spent its entire working life with that airline until it was retired in September 1994, after logging an impressive 95,000 flying hours. Captured on final approach to London-Heathrow in April 1981, it looks resplendent in the livery introduced the year before.

Scott Henderson

Lower right: TWA's bold red scheme, introduced on a 747 on 30 November 1974, first featured red outlined titles as seen here on -131 N53116. Five years later, more visible solid red titles were adopted fleet-wide.

Michael Gilliand

Originally delivered to Iran Air in March 1977, 747-286B Combi EP-IAH 'Khorasan' is seen on approach to London-Heathrow in April 1983. The aircraft, the 300th 747 built, is still in service today with the airline of the Islamic Republic of Iran.

George Ditchfield Collection

The Imperial Iranian Air Force bought a dozen ex-Continental and TWA 747-100s via Boeing in 1975, of which all but two were modified with SCDs to become -100SFs (Special Freighters). This is the first ex-TWA -131 to be delivered, 5-280, which later became 5-8101 and also used the civil registrations EP-NHJ and -NHV when leased by Iran Air.

Garuda, the state-owned airline of Indonesia, purchased six JT9D-powered 747-2U3Bs, the first four of which were delivered in 1980. In a then-record seating configuration for no less than 546 passengers, they were first used for that year's Hajj movement between Indonesia and Jeddah. All were named after Indonesian cities, illustrated by PK-GSB 'City of Bandung'.

Author's Collection

In September 1985, Garuda Indonesian Airways unveiled a new image as Garuda Indonesia, featuring the country's national bird from which the airline takes its name. 'City of Bandung' displays the revised colours on approach to London-Heathrow in June 1995.

P J Cooper

Polar Air Cargo, formed in 1990 by ex-Flying Tigers executives, started service in July 1994. It's entire fleet of a dozen -100s are converted passenger aircraft with SCDs. It also has a converted -200B, plus two ex-Flying Tigers -249Fs. Originally delivered to Delta Air Lines, 747-132 N857FT prepares to leave Manchester in June 1996.

George Ditchfield

Air Algérie titles were first applied to a 747 in 1975, when a World Airways -273C (N748WA) was chartered for Hajj flights. Another World -273C, N747WR, was leased for a year from April 1980 and was painted in Air Algérie colours, as seen here at Paris-Orly. Air Algérie came close to buying two ex-Braniff 747-227Bs in 1983, but although painted in the airline's new colours, they were never delivered.

George Ditchfield Collection

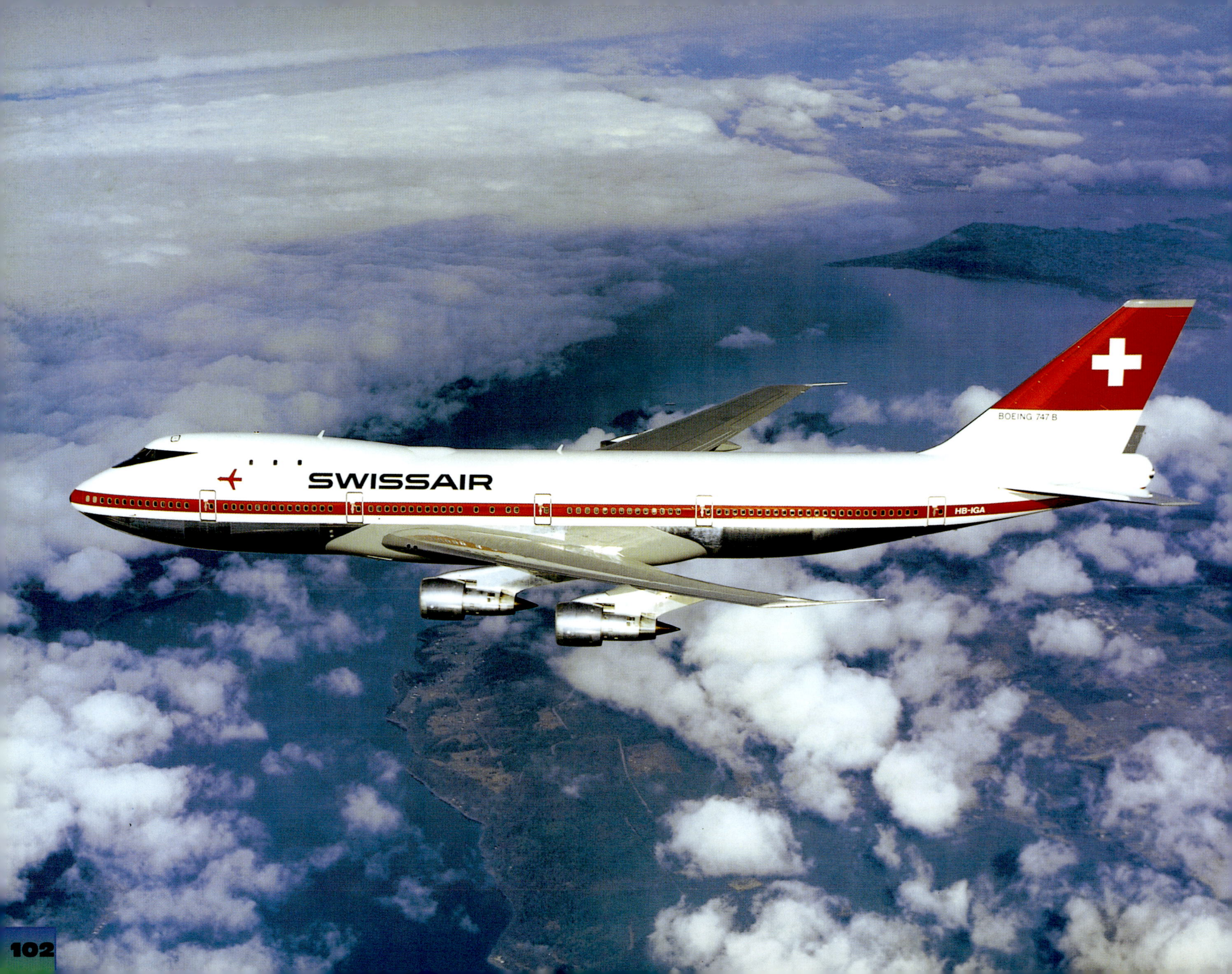
SWISSAIR
BOEING 747 B
HB-IGA

Left: In 1971, Swissair took delivery of two 353-seat 747-257Bs, mainly for its Zürich — Geneva — New York route. The first JT9D-powered aircraft, HB-IGA 'Genève', is seen here in its original colours.

Boeing

Top right: At Manchester in February 1978, HB-IGB 'Zürich' is being prepared for return to Switzerland after a fog diversion from London-Heathrow.

George Ditchfield

Lower right: A new livery was introduced by Swissair in 1979, depicted by the 747-257B flagship, HB-IGA 'Genève', caught on push-back at Zürich in July 1982. Both of Swissair's -200Bs were retired at the end of 1983 after four 747-300s had been delivered.

Author's Collection

Air New Zealand flies one of the longest air routes in the world, from Auckland to Los Angeles, then on to London. The tail fins of its fleet carry the 'Koru', a traditional Maori symbol. One of its RB211-powered 747-219Bs, ZK-NZW 'Tainui', prepares to land at London-Heathrow in February 1992 after one of its 26-hour marathons, half-way around the world.

Scott Henderson

Until it took delivery of its own 747-300s in 1988, EgyptAir operated a different 747 every year from 1983. This is its first aircraft, an ex-Lufthansa and Braniff 747-130, N480GX 'Cleopatra', leased from GATX between May 1983 and May 1984, and seen here at Tokyo-Narita.
K Murai via George Ditchfield Collection

Atlas Air is now the largest operator of cargo 747s, with a fleet of nineteen 747-200 freighters and five 747-400Fs, with five more on order. This ex-Air France 747-128, N3203Y, taken at Miami in June 1994, is now with Polar Air Cargo.

Scott Henderson

The Chinese state airline Air China, previously known as CAAC (Civil Aviation Administration of China), took delivery of the first of three 747-2J6Bs in December 1983. Long-haul passenger duties have now been taken over by 747-400s and Combi B-2446, seen above in May 1990, has recently been converted to a freighter, as will the other two aircraft.

George Ditchfield Collection

Malaysian Airline System (MAS) acquired two ex-British Airways RB211-powered 747-236Bs which were introduced in 1982 on its Kuala Lumpur — London route. The first aircraft was 9M-MHI 'Kuching', seen here in a fine air-to-air study. Both aircraft have since been converted to freighters for use by MASkargo.

Boeing

In November 1987, MAS changed its colour scheme and adopted simple 'Malaysia' titles to increase the awareness of the airline with its home country. The new livery is shown off by this 747-219B which was leased from Air New Zealand for twenty months from February 1991.

Author's Collection

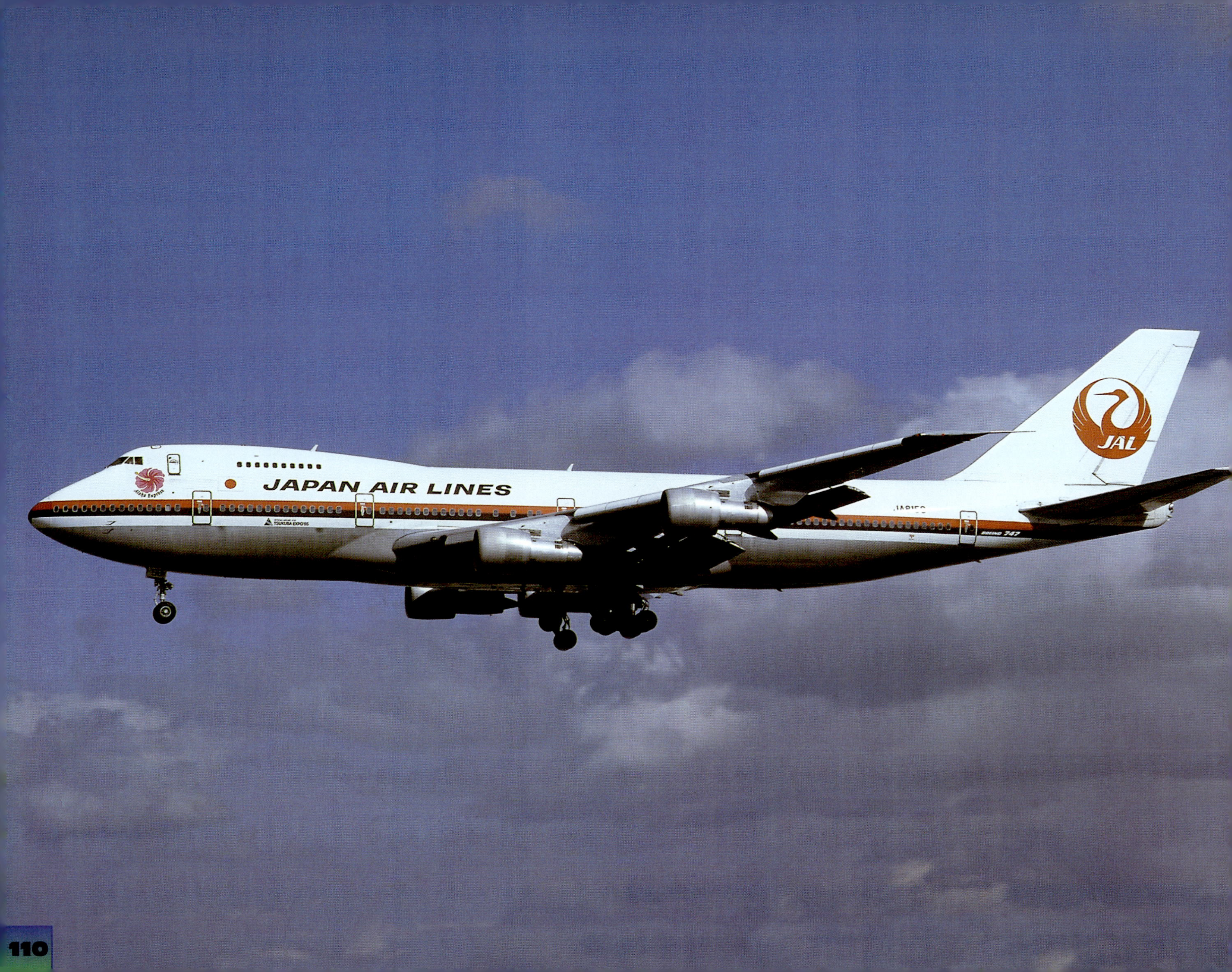
JAPAN AIR LINES
JAL

Left: With nearly eighty aircraft, Japan Airlines has the world's largest fleet of Boeing 747s to serve its world-wide network. This JT9D-powered 747-246B, JA8150, seen on approach to Osaka in November 1983, is one of a handful which carried 'Aloha Express' titles for charter flights to Hawaii.
K Murai via George Ditchfield

Top right: Cargo forms an important part of JAL's operation and JAL Cargo has a dedicated fleet of eight 747-200 freighters. The polished aluminium finish shown on -246F JA8180 on approach to Los Angeles has now been superseded by a 'Super Logistics' colour scheme.
Scott Henderson

Lower right: The current JAL colours are displayed by 747-146B (SR) JA8143 at Tokyo-Narita. One of only two such 533-seat Short Range models in the JAL fleet, it is normally assigned to the Tokyo — Osaka route, one of the busiest in the world.
P M Lammers via George Ditchfield

Famed entrepreneur Richard Branson founded Virgin Atlantic Airways in 1984 to compete with British Airways on North Atlantic routes. The airline has since become a global force and now operates a fleet of 747-400s, -200Bs, and one -123. This is G-VMIA, named 'Spirit of Sir Freddie' in tribute to the man who revolutionised UK air travel, which is seen here at Manchester in December 1991.

George Ditchfield

In the revised colours of Virgin Atlantic, introduced in November 1993, ex-QANTAS 747-238B G-VLAX 'California Girl', strikes a dramatic pose on approach to London-Heathrow in November 1997. The 'No Way BA/AA' slogan protests the proposed alliance between British Airways and American Airlines.

Bob Holder

China Airlines of Taiwan has been a 747 operator for twenty-three years. Purchased new, 747-209B B-1886 is one of three JT9D-powered -200s which will be converted to freighters for the airline's Dynasty Cargo division.

Author's Collection

China Airlines's Dynasty Cargo operation uses two -209Fs ordered in 1979, plus a converted -209B Combi for world-wide freight operations. One of the former aircraft, B-160, delivered in 1989, gradually loses height on approach to Hong Kong's now-closed Kai Tak.

George Ditchfield Collection

South African Airways introduced 747s on its London route in December 1971. Its flying springbok emblem and national blue, white, and orange colours are displayed on a pair of -244Bs at Johannesburg in April 1972.

Peter Keating

With the end of apartheid came the relaxation of restrictions upon South Africa's flag carrier and a striking new image was introduced, featuring the 'Horizon Mark', derived from the national flag with a golden arrow signifying precision. One of SAA's original 747-244Bs, ZS-SAM 'Drakensberg', looks resplendent in the livery at London-Heathrow during summer 1997.

Author's Collection

Scandinavian Airlines System, the airline jointly owned by Denmark, Norway, and Sweden, operated a total of six 747-283Bs between 1971 and 1987. Frequently, the aircraft were operated for SAS's charter subsidiary, Scanair. 'Ivar Viking' (OY-KHA) awaits its next turn of duty at Stockholm-Arlanda in May 1981.

George Ditchfield Collection

Cargolux ordered two JT9D-powered 747-2R7Fs in December 1977 to begin to replace its DC-8s. When LX-DCV 'City of Luxembourg', was delivered in January 1979, it gave Cargolux the distinction of being the first European all-cargo airline to operate the 747. Here we see the first aircraft in a rare quiet moment at Vancouver in August 1986.

George Ditchfield

Leased for seven months from British Airways from March 1984 for trans-Atlantic charters, 747-236B G-BDXL 'City of Winchester' of British Airtours makes a fine sight taxiing to the runway at Manchester.

George Ditchfield